I07951137

Gratitude
IS YOUR
SUPERPOWER

Gratitude IS YOUR SUPER POWER

A Book About Being Thankful and Embracing Positivity

WRITTEN BY
Amy Weber, LCSW

ILLUSTRATED BY
Zach Grzeszkowiak

ROCKRIDGE
PRESS

Copyright © 2022 by Rockridge Press, Oakland, California

No part of this publication may be reproduced, stored in a retrieval system, or transmitted in any form or by any means, electronic, mechanical, photocopying, recording, scanning, or otherwise, except as permitted under Sections 107 or 108 of the 1976 United States Copyright Act, without the prior written permission of the Publisher. Requests to the Publisher for permission should be addressed to the Permissions Department, Rockridge Press, 1955 Broadway, Suite 400, Oakland, CA 94612.

Limit of Liability/Disclaimer of Warranty: The Publisher and the author make no representations or warranties with respect to the accuracy or completeness of the contents of this work and specifically disclaim all warranties, including without limitation warranties of fitness for a particular purpose. No warranty may be created or extended by sales or promotional materials. The advice and strategies contained herein may not be suitable for every situation. This work is sold with the understanding that the Publisher is not engaged in rendering medical, legal, or other professional advice or services. If professional assistance is required, the services of a competent professional person should be sought. Neither the Publisher nor the author shall be liable for damages arising herefrom. The fact that an individual, organization, or website is referred to in this work as a citation and/or potential source of further information does not mean that the author or the Publisher endorses the information the individual, organization, or website may provide or recommendations they/it may make. Further, readers should be aware that websites listed in this work may have changed or disappeared between when this work was written and when it is read.

For general information on our other products and services or to obtain technical support, please contact our Customer Care Department within the United States at (866) 744-2665, or outside the United States at (510) 253-0500.

Rockridge Press publishes its books in a variety of electronic and print formats. Some content that appears in print may not be available in electronic books, and vice versa.

TRADEMARKS: Rockridge Press and the Rockridge Press logo are trademarks or registered trademarks of Callisto Media Inc. and/or its affiliates, in the United States and other countries, and may not be used without written permission. All other trademarks are the property of their respective owners. Rockridge Press is not associated with any product or vendor mentioned in this book.

Series Designer: Angie Chiu
Interior and Cover Designer: Jenny Paredes
Art Producer: Sara Feinstein
Editor: Jeanann Pannasch
Production Editor: Holland Baker
Production Manager: Martin Worthington

Illustration © 2022 Zachary Grzeszkowiak

Paperback ISBN: 978-1-63878-398-5
eBook ISBN: 978-1-63878-556-9
R0
Printed in China

For Alexander, Julia, and Sam.
I am so grateful to be your aunt!

We are all born with superpowers! Isn't that great?

You're about to meet best friends Grace and Guillermo, who have a superpower called gratitude.

And here's some greater news: With some observing, imagining, and feeling, **you** can have the superpower of gratitude, too.

Have you ever said "thank you" when someone gave you a cup of water?

Then you've already started building your gratitude superpowers!

Gratitude means noticing the people and things around you, and showing and telling them you are thankful.

Being thankful not only makes people feel great about themselves, it makes them feel happy, too. Showing our gratitude also helps build stronger friendships.

Can you think of a time when you noticed someone helping you?
How did you show them you were thankful for their help?

Grace first learned about gratitude when her family went on a hike. Grace's dad told her he was thankful they were all together in the beautiful forest. Grace agreed and said, "I'm thankful, too. Spending time with our family, and looking at the trees and mountains, makes me so happy."

What was Grace's dad thankful for?
What about Grace?
Look around. What do you see to be thankful for?

We all have lots of different feelings.

Sometimes we feel happy or silly.

Other times we feel angry or sad.

Sometimes we make mistakes, and that's okay.

When you have the gratitude superpower, you get to decide how you feel. Instead of being upset over losing a baseball game, for example, you can be grateful you got to enjoy time outside with friends!

Is it sometimes hard to change your mood when you're feeling sad or angry?

Have you ever been able to feel grateful even if something didn't turn out as you expected?

Everyone is different—and this is something to be grateful for! Grace and Guillermo know they can learn to appreciate new things through their differences. By expressing gratitude, they can make everyone around them feel good.

Let's see how they practice their gratitude superpower every day.

Can you name some things you've learned from friends who are different from you?

What are ways you can show gratitude to friends who have taught you new things?

At Grace's birthday party,

Ming noticed a pile of big gifts.

She felt embarrassed that her

gift was smaller than the others.

But after Grace opened Ming's gift, Ming was relieved. "Unicorns are my favorite," Grace exclaimed. "Thank you, Ming! I can tell you worked hard on this picture. I love it!" Ming beamed with pride.

How did Grace use her gratitude superpower? What would you say if someone gave you a handmade birthday gift?

Emma and Guillermo were riding scooters

when Guillermo fell down and scraped his elbow.

He started to cry.

Emma ran inside to get a bandage and helped put it on his arm. Then she gave him a hug. "Thank you, Emma!" Guillermo said. "You helped me feel better!"

How did Guillermo use his gratitude superpower?

How do you feel when someone tells you "thank you"?

While playing at Grace's house, Grace wanted to show Mateo her special pillow. But where was it?

Mateo said he would help Grace look around.

They found it under her bed. Grace thanked him and said, "I'm so glad you helped me find my pillow—it's my favorite!"

How did Grace use her gratitude superpower? What do you do when someone helps you find something?

Guillermo and Emmanuel were reading partners in school. One day, the words were a little tricky for Guillermo to figure out. Emmanuel noticed Guillermo was frustrated, so he said, "Let's do this together."

Emmanuel then helped his friend sound out the difficult words. "Thanks for slowing down and helping me, Emmanuel," Guillermo said with a smile.

How did Guillermo use his gratitude superpower? How do you feel when someone takes time to help you?

Grace noticed Emma sitting alone at the base of a tree. Emma looked sad and lonely, so Grace went over and asked her to join her and other friends playing freeze tag.

Emma answered,

"Thank you, Grace!

I'd love to join you!"

How did Emma use her gratitude superpower?

How do you feel when someone invites you to play?

Ming could see Guillermo was nervous before his turn at the spelling bee. She took off her lucky dolphin pendant, handed it to him, and said, “Mimi can keep you company. You are doing great!

“Thank you, Ming,” said Guillermo, as he put the necklace on. It gave him the confidence he needed to be ready for his turn.

How did Guillermo use his gratitude superpower? Have you ever been grateful because someone helped you do something difficult?

When it suddenly started raining, Carlos and Grace pulled out their umbrellas.

They noticed Clara was struggling to carry a project to class, and the rain was getting it all wet.

Grace and Carlos offered to share their umbrellas with Clara to help keep her and her project dry.

Clara eagerly said,

"Thank you both!

I really appreciate your help!"

How did Clara use her gratitude superpower? How does it feel when someone shares something with you?

Guillermo was excited for his dance recital.

The class has been practicing hard!

Guillermo's parents, sister, little brother, aunt, uncle, and

grandparents were there to watch the show.

Afterward, Guillermo thanked them all for coming to the show. He told them, "I am so grateful to have such a supportive family!"

How did Guillermo use his gratitude superpower?
Have you ever thanked someone for coming to watch your sports game or your class show?

As Mateo, Carlos, and Grace were creating posters for their school carnival, Carlos got frustrated when his picture wasn't coming out as he imagined.

Mateo stopped coloring his poster to help Carlos. Carlos then started to feel better about his drawing and smiled. Grace saw what a good friend Mateo was being to Carlos, and she also smiled. "I'm grateful we're such a great team!" Grace exclaimed.

How did Grace use her gratitude superpower? How do you feel when you see people help each other?

Feeling and expressing gratitude made Grace and Guillermo feel good, and others, too! Grace thanked Ming for the beautiful picture, and that made Ming feel happy. Guillermo was grateful for his loving family.
Emma was thankful that Grace invited her to join the group playing freeze tag.

You can spread gratitude, too, when you use your own gratitude superpower to make people happy. It will make you feel good, too!

What are some things you could do to show your gratitude?
Can you name people or things that you feel grateful for right now?

for **PARENTS, EDUCATORS,** *and* **CAREGIVERS**

Gratitude Superpower Practice!

Tips and Activities That Help Kids Cultivate Gratitude, Give Thanks, and Be Grateful

At times, teaching gratitude might feel like an uphill battle, but it truly is a superpower! Research shows that instilling a sense of gratitude in young children leads to increased happiness, a greater sense of optimism, and better social supports. In adolescence, this can mean teens that are more engaged in school work, have better grades, and are active members of their families and communities.

Gratitude is more complex than just teaching kids to say "thank you," although that is a wonderful place to start. It begins with *noticing*—recognizing the things and people (and pets!) in your life to be grateful for. It then involves *thinking*—reflecting on why you have been given those things; *feeling*—how you feel about the things you've been given; and *doing*—how you can show gratitude for them.

Gratitude is a muscle that needs to be exercised regularly to reap the benefits.

Ready to start practicing?

Create a Gratitude Jar

Decorate the outside of a jar, such as a cleaned-out plastic peanut butter jar. Set aside markers, paper, glue, paint—whatever supplies you have on hand. At least once week, on ice cream sticks or slips of paper, have your child write or draw things that they are grateful for, and add them to the jar. When you see your child adding to the jar, praise them, and discuss it. You should add to the jar, too, narrating your actions. At the end of the week (or month), read all the statements from the jar out loud to the whole family. Honor all the good things happening in your lives.

Superpower Practice!

Ask your child to add to the jar whenever they are grateful. Help point out occasions that they may have missed. Encourage them to consider the big and small moments. Label your own gratitude as often as possible so that it becomes common language in your home.

Discussion Questions

How does it feel to notice what you're thankful for?
Did you express your gratitude in the moment?
How does it feel to hear about good things that are happening in someone else's life?
Can your family spread gratitude?
What do you think about the good things that happened today?

Take a Gratitude Walk

Go for a walk through your neighborhood with the specific intention of noticing things to be grateful for. If your child has a hard time getting started, model for them. For example, "I am so thankful for this tree! It gives us shade when we're outside, and it helps give us air to breathe." Or "I'm so thankful to be spending time with you today! We're both so busy, and it's nice to slow down and enjoy our time together."

Superpower Practice!

This is another great time to model for your kids and encourage them to notice the big and small things. It is also an opportunity to go a little deeper by asking them the same key questions: What do they think about the things they're noticing? How do these people and things make them feel? How might they like to show their gratitude?

Discussion Questions

How many things did you notice today to be grateful for?
Did it get harder, or easier, to notice things during your walk? Why?
How can you show your gratitude?
How does it feel to be thankful?
Can you feel gratitude in your body? Where?

Start a Gratitude Ritual

Start a routine at dinnertime (or before bed, in the morning—anytime works!) where each person names one thing from the day that they're grateful for. This is great to practice the four parts of gratitude: noticing, thinking, feeling, doing. What do you *notice* around you to be grateful for? What do you *think* about that? How does it make you *feel*? What can you *do* to show gratitude?

Superpower Practice!

What a welcoming way to turn dinner conversation into a positive reflection on the events and people of the day. It might be tough to do at first (gratitude is a muscle, after all!), but it will become easier and less forced as you practice. As always, it is important for you to model; if your child is having trouble getting started, you can begin with an example from your day.

Discussion Questions

Is it easy to remember recent, new things you're grateful for?

What have you been given that isn't a material object, like someone helping you, or someone showing that they care?

What did you do to express your gratitude today? During your day did you notice anyone else expressing gratitude?

How does it feel to hear about what others are thankful for?

A Note of Gratitude

Each time your child receives a gift, insist on written thank-you notes. If they aren't able to write on their own yet, they can draw a picture or dictate while you write for them. Already doing that, and ready to level up? Write thank-you notes to people in the community that help you: mail carrier, grocery store worker, librarian, police officer, doctor or nurse, firefighter. The possibilities are endless!

Superpower Practice!

In a time when emails/texts/video calls are our typical methods of communication, it is really a gift to send and receive letters. Wait for a time when your child is calm and suggest writing a brief note. Follow their lead on how to complete the letter and respect their wishes if they say they want to do it later. (You definitely do not want gratitude to feel burdensome!)

Discussion Questions

How does it feel to write these notes?
How do you think the person receiving the note feels when they read it?
Why did this person give you a gift?
Does anyone owe you a gift? What are reasons that people give gifts?
Why does this person help people in our community?

Gratitude in Action

Think of a goodwill project close to home where your child could participate. It can be a small act of kindness, such as cheering up a neighbor by expressing your gratitude for them. As an example, the next time you are baking cookies with your child, you could make some extra to drop off to that neighbor. If a relative could use some help with yard work, pick a weekend to go over with rakes and leaf bags. Get creative and have some fun with it!

Superpower Practice!

This is a great opportunity to get your child involved in noticing who may need help or thinking about how they can show gratitude beyond saying thank you. Maybe a friend lent your child a toy, and your child can return the favor, or a relative who always comes to your child's soccer games can be helped in some way. Be sure to call out you are "returning the favor," such as "Guillermo always comes to your piano recitals. Let's show him how thankful we are by doing something kind for him. What do you think he'd like? Should we go to one of his basketball games? Invite him to dinner?"

Discussion Questions

How does it feel to do something for someone else?
What does it mean to spread gratitude?
How do you think the other person will feel?
Why are you doing something kind for someone else?
Do you think the other person will feel grateful? How might they show it?

Family Gratitude Book

Using a scrapbook or empty binder and a pile of old magazines (or images printed from your phone/computer), cut out pictures or words of things that represent what makes you feel grateful. Glue them into the scrapbook, or onto paper to put into the binder. Add to the book at least once a month, and discuss the pages that you've already completed.

Superpower Practice!

This is a great exercise for helping your child think beyond pictures of toys they have and/or want and instead think about bigger ideas. Examples might include "family," "having a best friend," or "being able to read chapter books now." This is another opportunity to lead by example and focus on those ideas when cutting out your own pictures or words.

Discussion Questions

What kinds of things are we noticing to be grateful for?
Can you think of things that aren't objects that you're thankful for?
How does it feel to look at these pictures?
Can you think of different ways to express gratitude for these things/people?
Why are you grateful for this particular person/thing?

Look for the Silver Lining

Instead of dwelling on disappointing moments, point out the silver lining. For example, if your child's soccer game was rained out, point out that you can now use the time to watch a movie together while staying cozy and dry. If a friend is moving away, you could say, "I'm sad that Grace is moving, but I'm grateful that we were able to be friends with her and her family for the last two years."

Superpower Practice!

This activity can be tough for kids in the moment, and you don't want to dismiss their genuine feelings of disappointment or sadness. If your child is upset, it's best to acknowledge/label that feeling and help them "regulate" (return to a peaceful, relaxed state). Later, when they're calm and reconnected to you, you can look for the positive in the upsetting situation. If they cannot see it, that's fine! The idea is to introduce this concept and practice it as you can.

Discussion Questions

What's something good that could come out of something bad?
Can you be happy and sad/mad/disappointed at the same time?
How does it feel to be grateful in this situation?
Can you think of other times when something good came out of something bad?
How does thinking about the silver lining affect your mood?

Resources

BucketFillers101.com
Bucket Fillers 101 is filled with ideas for promoting kindness for parents and educators. Find videos of read-alouds, free printable materials, gratitude journal prompts, and more.

CASEL.org
The Collaborative for Academic, Social, and Emotional Learning is a nonprofit organization for educators, therapists, policy makers, and parents on advancing social and emotional learning in our classrooms, communities, and homes.

CommonSenseMedia.org/character-strengths-and-life-skills/what-is-gratitude
Common Sense Media is an indispensable resource for parents and educators, providing reviews and information about all forms of media that kids are exposed to every day. They have a section on using media to teach gratitude.

CSEFEL.vanderbilt.edu/index.html
The Center on the Social and Emotional Foundations for Early Learning at Vanderbilt University provides research, training, and materials to promote social-emotional learning at home, in schools, and in communities.

LearningforJustice.org
Learning for Justice provides free resources and materials about creating inclusive school communities for educators who work with children in grades K to 12.

PBSkids.org/grownups
PBS is a nonprofit organization dedicated to using media to educate and entertain. Their website is filled with activities, videos, and digital resources for parents and educators.

PositivePsychology.com/gratitude-tree-kids
Positive Psychology provides free resources to therapists, teachers, and administrators. They have free printable gratitude activities.

WeAreTeachers.com/gratitude-videos
We Are Teachers is a website filled with classroom strategies, teaching ideas, and actionable tips for teachers. They have 22 different (free!) videos about gratitude for children as well as free printable activities.

Acknowledgments

No book about gratitude would be complete without an acknowledgment of my own gratitude. I am thankful for my editor, Jeanann Pannasch, who was patient and nurturing through this entire process. I am grateful for my friends, especially Anne, Maria, Christi, and Kate, who encouraged me to take on this project and supported me every step of the way. I am indebted to my parents, who model gratitude and generosity every day. I am appreciative of my siblings, Jill and Patrick, for teaching me perseverance, humor, and creativity. And I am most thankful for my husband, Marc. I could not imagine a more supportive, loving, adventurous, hilarious partner to walk through life with.

About the Author

Amy's teacher once told her to look for a job that made her feel excited every day. And she was lucky enough to find one—being a therapist and feelings teacher for kids!

Amy Weber, LCSW, has over 25 years of experience working with children and their families as both a clinician and administrator. Amy imparts her passion for play and social-emotional learning in her private practice, where she sees children and adolescents. She is a cofounder of Speak, Learn, & Play in Brooklyn, New York, where she shares space and ideas with a group of brilliant pediatric therapists. Amy also provides training and consultation to schools and agencies throughout New York City, and is in the process of publishing her innovative group therapy curriculum for other practitioners. When not playing and traveling the world, Amy lives with her husband in Brooklyn. She hopes to someday have a dog and to finish all of her quilt projects.

About the Illustrator

Zach Grzeszkowiak is a graphic designer and illustrator originally from the Chicagoland area. He creates both digital and printed marketing materials like logos, infographics, and catalogs. In addition to his responsibilities as a designer, Zach also enjoys illustrating, animating, and sculpting colorful and exciting characters. Some of his favorite things to draw are animals and spooky creatures. He is constantly improving his skill set by drawing every day and experimenting with new mediums to work with. His favorite types of projects to work on involve educating, storytelling, and promoting positive change. To him, there's nothing quite as rewarding as using your talents and strengths to help a cause that you care deeply about.

What *Superpower* Will You Learn Next?

Get the whole series and
explore more skills that make kids super.

Look for this series wherever books and ebooks are sold.

DISCOVER THE POWER OF FEELINGS

Empathy Is Your Superpower
Confidence Is Your Superpower
Gratitude Is Your Superpower
Mindfulness Is Your Superpower